Instant jQuery 2.0 Table Manipulation How-to

Enhance and add functionality with interactivity to your HTML tables with jQuery

Charlie Griefer

BIRMINGHAM - MUMBAI

Instant jQuery 2.0 Table Manipulation How-to

First published: March 2013

Production Reference: 1200313

Published by Packt Publishing Ltd.
Livery Place
35 Livery Street
Birmingham B3 2PB, UK.

ISBN 978-1-78216-468-5

www.packtpub.com

Credits

Author
Charlie Griefer

Reviewer
Victoria Ryder

Acquisition Editor
Martin Bell

Commissioning Editor
Ameya Sawant

Technical Editor
Sharvari Baet

Project Coordinator
Sherin Padayatty

Proofreader
Aaron Nash

Production Coordinator
Arvindkumar Gupta

Cover Work
Arvindkumar Gupta

Cover Image
Conidon Miranda

About the Author

Charlie Griefer has been building websites and applications since 1996, which makes him 217 years old in Internet years.

A native of New Jersey, he moved to Phoenix in 1995, where he resided for 10 years before going on a whirlwind tour of the country in search of happiness or something similar. Short stints in Florida, California (lower), and California (upper) ultimately led to his return to Phoenix in 2010.

Charlie is currently a Senior Web Applications Developer at World Singles, where his day-to-day activities include CFML, Clojure, JavaScript, jQuery, MySQL, MongoDB, and grudgingly, some CSS.

When he's not in front of the computer working on code, he can be found in front of the computer playing with code.

When he's not in front of the computer at all, he enjoys spending time with his wife and three children, or trying to survive Krav Maga classes. He infrequently blogs at `http://charlie.griefer.com/blog`.

I am grateful for this opportunity and want to say *thank you* to everybody at World Singles. I'm humbled to be associated with such an incredible and wonderful group of people. You've all helped me see that life is, in a word, good.

Within that group, I have to single out my manager, Sean Corfield. You challenge me, you encourage me, you teach me, and you motivate me. If I am a better programmer today than I was yesterday, it's because of you. It is both an honor and a privilege, and I am forever in your debt.

Of course, none of it would matter without my wife, Becky, by my side. You have sacrificed much and spent far too much time alone while I built a career. Yet you've stuck by my side throughout this crazy ride. You are the light that eradicates my darkness. If I am a better husband and father today than I was yesterday, if I'm a better man today than I was yesterday, it's because of you. One love, one lifetime. I cross my heart.

About the Reviewer

Victoria Ryder has been a web applications developer for over a decade and has been applying her technical knowledge to a variety of innovative projects and purposes. Most recently, she owns and operates CodeBass Radio (http://www.codebassradio.net), an Internet radio station whose core team is comprised of developers, designers, and other knowledgeable industry experts.

I would like to thank my loving husband, Martin Ryder, for putting up with my insanity while I do bizarre things, such as tech review books and stuff.

www.PacktPub.com

Support files, eBooks, discount offers and more

You might want to visit www.PacktPub.com for support files and downloads related to your book.

Did you know that Packt offers eBook versions of every book published, with PDF and ePub files available? You can upgrade to the eBook version at www.PacktPub.com and as a print book customer, you are entitled to a discount on the eBook copy. Get in touch with us at service@packtpub.com for more details.

At www.PacktPub.com, you can also read a collection of free technical articles, sign up for a range of free newsletters and receive exclusive discounts and offers on Packt books and eBooks.

http://PacktLib.PacktPub.com

Do you need instant solutions to your IT questions? PacktLib is Packt's online digital book library. Here, you can access, read and search across Packt's entire library of books.

Why Subscribe?

- ▶ Fully searchable across every book published by Packt
- ▶ Copy and paste, print and bookmark content
- ▶ On demand and accessible via web browser

Free Access for Packt account holders

If you have an account with Packt at www.PacktPub.com, you can use this to access PacktLib today and view nine entirely free books. Simply use your login credentials for immediate access.

Table of Contents

Preface

"Table manipulation?" you ask. "But why would anybody be using tables? Aren't tables in HTML bad?"

Tables get a bit of an unfair shake nowadays. They used to be the sledgehammer of HTML. Page layouts were done fully in tables. It used to be the right tool for the job. Actually, it was the only tool.

Then CSS started to gain popularity. Tables for layouts were replaced with divs, floats, and positioning. CSS was certainly a better option for page layout by orders of magnitude. It allowed for more modular design. It became easier to reuse page fragments. It became easier to update and change different areas of the page without having to modify a monolithic containing table and in many cases various nested tables. Tables quickly became shunned in favor of the more elegant CSS option.

But rather than just being shunned for page layouts, tables became shunned altogether. I recall seeing blog entries where people proudly posted CSS alternatives to using tables for displaying the tabular data. Complex combinations of divs and floats were simply not necessary. When it comes to displaying tabular data, HTML tables should be the delivery mechanism of choice. While tables were never truly meant to be used for page layouts, and moving to CSS there makes sense, they are certainly meant to be used to display tabular data. If you need to display rows and columns of data, not only are HTML tables acceptable, but they're really the proper choice.

What this book covers

Table row striping (Must know) explains how to apply colors to alternating table rows without making any modifications to your HTML.

Sum columns (Must know) explains how to dynamically calculate the total of a table column that contains numeric variables. This is handy for database-driven pages where the values to be added are not static.

Show/hide rows (Must know) explains how to organize data in your tables and allow users to determine what they want see and what they don't. They'll be able to click on a link to show or hide specified table rows.

Highlighting cells (Must know) explains how to add functionality to your tables by quickly and easily highlighting cells that contain specific data. Any number of colors can be used, making it easy to group related bits of information as well.

Pagination – client side (Should know) explains how to organize the content and allow users to page through the data at their own pace rather than overwhelming your users with rows upon rows of table data.

Pagination – server side (Should know) is similar to the previous recipe, but more efficient. It explains how to request only for the data that you intend to display, rather than loading and then hiding data that you don't want. Use AJAX to request only specific records to display.

Column Sorting – client side (Should know) explains how to add interactivity to your tables by allowing users to sort data in a way that's most meaningful to them. Easily make any table sortable by column.

Column Sorting – server side (Should know) explains how it's sometimes better to do the manipulation on the server if your tables are displaying many rows of data. Use AJAX and your database to return data already sorted as per the user's request.

Filtering (Become an expert) explains how column sorting and paging can go a long way towards helping users organize data. But nothing cuts to the chase like allowing them to filter out all data that does not meet specific criteria.

Plugins (Should know) explains how the power of jQuery comes in its extensibility through plugins. Look at two powerful and popular jQuery plugins that will help make your HTML tables pop!

What you need for this book

At the very minimum, you'll need a text editor and a browser. Most of the recipes won't need to be run on a web server, other than the two recipes that incorporate AJAX. For the others, you can simply save your `.html` files and use your browser of choice to open them locally.

At a maximum, you'll want a web server (for example, Microsoft IIS, Apache, Nginx) and a database (for example, SQL Server, MySQL, PostGreSQL).

Who this book is for

If you can write HTML, this book is for you. Even if you've never written a lick of jQuery, you can copy and paste the jQuery code provided to you. If it doesn't work as desired out-of-the-box, it should be fairly simple to make the necessary tweaks to fulfill your specific requirements.

While the purpose of this book isn't to teach jQuery, I've tried to explain how the code works, so even jQuery novices should be able to work comfortably with the sample code.

Conventions

In this book, you will find a number of styles of text that distinguish between different kinds of information. Here are some examples of these styles, and an explanation of their meaning.

Code words in text are shown as follows: "We can include other contexts through the use of the `include` directive."

A block of code is set as follows:

```
<tr>
  <th>Header Data 1</th>
  <th>Header Data 2</th>
</tr>
```

When we wish to draw your attention to a particular part of a code block, the relevant lines or items are set in bold:

```
<tr>
  <td>Footer Data 1</td>
  <td>Footer Data 2</td>
</tr>
```

New terms and **important words** are shown in bold. Words that you see on the screen, in menus or dialog boxes for example, appear in the text like this: "Clicking on the **Next** button moves you to the next screen."

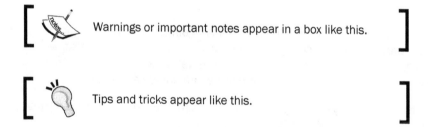

Warnings or important notes appear in a box like this.

Tips and tricks appear like this.

Reader feedback

Feedback from our readers is always welcome. Let us know what you think about this book— what you liked or may have disliked. Reader feedback is important for us to develop titles that you really get the most out of.

To send us general feedback, simply send an e-mail to `feedback@packtpub.com`, and mention the book title via the subject of your message.

If there is a topic that you have expertise in and you are interested in either writing or contributing to a book, see our author guide on www.packtpub.com/authors.

Customer support

Now that you are the proud owner of a Packt book, we have a number of things to help you to get the most from your purchase.

Downloading the example code

You can download the example code files for all Packt books you have purchased from your account at http://www.packtpub.com. If you purchased this book elsewhere, you can visit http://www.packtpub.com/support and register to have the files e-mailed directly to you.

Errata

Although we have taken every care to ensure the accuracy of our content, mistakes do happen. If you find a mistake in one of our books—maybe a mistake in the text or the code— we would be grateful if you would report this to us. By doing so, you can save other readers from frustration and help us improve subsequent versions of this book. If you find any errata, please report them by visiting http://www.packtpub.com/submit-errata, selecting your book, clicking on the **errata submission form** link, and entering the details of your errata. Once your errata are verified, your submission will be accepted and the errata will be uploaded on our website, or added to any list of existing errata, under the Errata section of that title. Any existing errata can be viewed by selecting your title from http://www.packtpub.com/support.

Piracy

Piracy of copyright material on the Internet is an ongoing problem across all media. At Packt, we take the protection of our copyright and licenses very seriously. If you come across any illegal copies of our works, in any form, on the Internet, please provide us with the location address or website name immediately so that we can pursue a remedy.

Please contact us at copyright@packtpub.com with a link to the suspected pirated material.

We appreciate your help in protecting our authors, and our ability to bring you valuable content.

Questions

You can contact us at questions@packtpub.com if you are having a problem with any aspect of the book, and we will do our best to address it.

Instant jQuery 2.0 Table Manipulation How-to

In order to write effective jQuery, it's important to write well marked-up HTML. Browsers are generally forgiving, and will render most markup to the best of their abilities. But jQuery, which has been referred to as the "find-something/do-something" framework, accomplishes the "find-something" part with its powerful selector engine (see http://api.jquery.com/cateogry/selectors/).

For example, including `<thead>`, `<tbody>`, and `<tfoot>` tags in your table give jQuery direct access to those DOM elements. Consider the following table markup:

```
<table id="myTable">
<thead>
  <tr><th>Column 1</th></tr>
  <tr><th>Column 2</th></tr>
</thead>
<tfoot>
  <tr><td colspan="2">&copy; Charlie Griefer. So there!</td></tr>
</tfoot>
<tbody>
  <tr>
    <td class="firstColumn">Column 1 data</td>
    <td>Column 2 data</td>
  </tr>
  <tr>
    <td class="firstColumn">More Column 1 data</td>
    <td>More Column 2 data</td>
  </tr>
</tbody>
</table>
```

With the properly structured table, selecting the `<tr>` in the table footer is as simple as:

```
$( "#myTable tfoot tr" );
```

What this does is select the element with an ID of `myTable`, then selects that element's `<tfoot>`, and then `<tr>` within.

Without the `<tfoot>` tag, the selector would look more like:

```
$( "#myTable tr:last" );
```

While this selector doesn't look any worse, what it's doing is actually selecting all of the `<tr>` elements within the table, and then filtering out all but the last of the rows. This is inefficient at best. Why select all of the rows if you only want one?

Another aspect of well marked-up HTML that helps tremendously with jQuery is the use of **id** and **class** attributes.

An `id`, as the name implies, should identify a *unique* element. There should only be one ID of a given value on any particular page. The table in the preceding markup has an ID of `myTable`. Not particularly original, but descriptive. No other elements on the page should be assigned that ID.

A class, on the other hand, is reused and identifies a **group** of elements. The preceding markup shows that all of the `<td>` elements that make up the first column have a class of `firstColumn`. This would allow us to easily display all of the text in all cells in the first column in bold via:

```
$( "#myTable .firstColumn" ).css( "font-weight", "bold" );
```

Prefacing the class with the ID of the element is optional. The following code works as well:

```
$( ".firstColumn" ).css( "font-weight", "bold" );
```

But this code searches the entire page for any elements with the class of `firstColumn`. The first code sample is concerned only with elements inside of a specified element. This makes it more efficient.

Besides a well marked-up table, the only other thing you need to get started is jQuery itself.

Including jQuery into your pages is simple. You can either download it from `http://www.jquery.com/download/`, or include it from a CDN such as Google's or jQuery's.

All of the code samples in this book will include the beta version of jQuery 2.0 from jQuery's CDN. However, all of the recipes should work with any recent version of jQuery.

jQuery 2.0 should work with most modern browsers. See `http://jquery.com/browser-support/` for the list of supported browsers in both jQuery 2.0 as well as jQuery 1.9. If any of the code samples fail to run in your browser, please either update to a newer browser, or modify the code samples to include and use an older version of jQuery that supports your browser.

Table row striping (Must know)

In this section, we will add color to alternate rows so that we can easily distinguish between the table rows.

Getting ready

You will need a simple HTML table. The table can be written by hand in HTML, or generated by a client-side language, such as PHP. The beauty of the jQuery solution is that it is completely unobtrusive to the markup. Your sample table might look as follows:

Planet Name	Radius	Surface Area	Distance from Sun	Inhabitants Use jQuery
Mercury	1,516 miles (2,440 km)	74,800,000 km^2	35,980,000 miles (57,910,000 km)	No
Venus	3,760 miles (6,052 km)	460,200,000 km^2	67,240,000 miles (108,200,000 km)	No
Earth	3,959 miles (6,371 km)	510,100,000 km^2	92,960,000 miles (149,600,000 km)	YES
Mars	2,106 miles (3,389 km)	144,800,000 km^2	141,600,000 miles (227,900,000 km)	No
Jupiter	43,441 miles (69,911 km)	61,420,000,000 km^2	483,800,000 miles (778,500,000 km)	No
Saturn	36,184 miles (58,232 km)	42,610,000,000 km^2	890,700,000 miles (1,433,000,000 km)	No
Uranus	15,759 miles (25,362 km)	8,083,000,000 km^2	1,787,000,000 miles (2,877,000,000 km)	No
Neptune	15,299 miles (24,622 km)	7,618,000,000 km^2	2,798,000,000 miles (4,503,000,000 km)	No

How to do it...

1. Give the table an `id` attribute. As a general rule, most elements should have either `id` or `class` attributes, and many times both. This will make them easier to be selected via jQuery. For this recipe, give the table an `id` of `planetsTable`, `<table id="planetsTable">`.

2. Add some rows to the `tbody` as follows:

```
<tr>
  <td>Mercury</td>
  <td>1,516 miles (2,440 km)</td>
  <td>74,800,000 km<sup>2</sup></td>
  <td>35,980,000 miles (57,910,000 km)</td>
  <td>No</td>
</tr>
```

```
<tr>
    <td>Venus</td>
    <td>3,760 miles (6,052 km)</td>
    <td>460,200,000 km<sup>2</sup></td>
    <td>67,240,000 miles (108,200,000 km)</td>
    <td>No</td>
</tr>
```

Downloading the example code

You can download the example code files for all Packt books you have purchased from your account at http://www.packtpub.com. If you purchased this book elsewhere, you can visit http://www.packtpub.com/support and register to have the files e-mailed directly to you.

3. With the table in place, you can now write the jQuery to perform the row striping as follows:

```
<script type="text/javascript">
    $( document ).ready( function() {
        $( "#planetsTable tbody tr:even" ).css( "background-color",
          "#CECECE" );
    });
</script>
```

Now when the page is rendered, you should see a nicely striped table as shown in the following screenshot:

Planet Name	Radius	Surface Area	Distance from Sun	Inhabitants Use jQuery
Mercury	1,516 miles (2,440 km)	74,800,000 km^2	35,980,000 miles (57,910,000 km)	No
Venus	3,760 miles (6,052 km)	460,200,000 km^2	67,240,000 miles (108,200,000 km)	No
Earth	3,959 miles (6,371 km)	510,100,000 km^2	92,960,000 miles (149,600,000 km)	YES
Mars	2,106 miles (3,389 km)	144,800,000 km^2	141,600,000 miles (227,900,000 km)	No
Jupiter	43,441 miles (69,911 km)	61,420,000,000 km^2	483,800,000 miles (778,500,000 km)	No
Saturn	36,184 miles (58,232 km)	42,610,000,000 km^2	890,700,000 miles (1,433,000,000 km)	No
Uranus	15,759 miles (25,362 km)	8,083,000,000 km^2	1,787,000,000 miles (2,877,000,000 km)	No
Neptune	15,299 miles (24,622 km)	7,618,000,000 km^2	2,798,000,000 miles (4,503,000,000 km)	No

How it works...

This one-liner makes use of jQuery selectors to first find every even row within the tbody of the table with the planetsTable ID. ID values should be unique, so there should be only one.

An `id` attribute in jQuery is identified with a # character. `#planetsTable` tells jQuery to select that particular table, but you need to drill further down to get into the table rows.

The next piece of the selector is `tbody tr`. You've directed jQuery to select the table rows that are inside the `tbody` of the table with an ID of `planetsTable`. But you need to drill further down to get every other row.

The selected table rows are part of a collection. Applying the `:even` selector to the collection returns records whose index is even, starting with 0.

Reading back to front, you've selected every other table row (evens, in this case) that belong to the `tbody` of the table with the ID of `planetsTable`.

You have successfully *found* something. Now, you need to *do* something.

In this case, you're going to use jQuery's built-in `css()` method. The `css()` method, when used as a setter, takes two arguments. First, the CSS property to set, and second, the value to set. In this case, set the `background-color` property to #ECECEC. This is done via `.css( "background-color", "#ECECEC" )`.

Putting it all together, you have the following:

```
$( "#planetsTable tbody tr:even" ).css( "background-color", "#ECECEC"
);
```

There's more...

As with the `:even` selector, jQuery also has an `:odd` selector. They both work the same, so use whichever one looks more appealing to you.

Declaring a style inline, as in the `css()` method, is a bit of a "code smell". Styles should ideally be defined in classes in a valid `<style>` block or an external CSS file. With that in mind, let's see the following class declaration:

```
<style type="text/css">
  .trGrey { background-color: #ECECEC; }
</style>.
```

The table row colors can be manipulated with jQuery's built-in `addClass()` method:

```
$( "#planetsTable tbody tr:even" ).addClass( "trGrey" );
```

This allows the CSS, which is a style concern, to be modified without touching the jQuery, which is a code concern.

Sum columns (Must know)

This section shows us how to use jQuery to create an array of cells that make up a table column, add the values together, and display the total in the bottom-row.

Getting ready

You will need a simple HTML table (this will be a recurring theme under each *Getting ready* section). Make sure your table has a `<tfoot>` section with one row, which will hold the sums. Make sure your table has a `<tfoot>` section with one row, which will hold the sums.

Country	Population
Canada	34482779
China	1344130000
India	1241491960
Japan	127817277
United States	311591917

How to do it...

1. Once again, give the table an `id` attribute. The table should have a column of numeric values that can be added together.

   ```
   <table border="1" id="populationTable">
   ```

2. Add a `thead` and a few rows to the `tbody`, as follows:

   ```
   <thead>
     <tr>
       <th>Country</th>
       <th>Population</th>
     </tr>
   </thead>
   <tbody>
     <tr>
       <td>Canada</td>
       <td class="numeric">34482779</td>
     </tr>
     <tr>
       <td>China</td>
       <td class="numeric">1344130000</td>
     </tr>
   </tbody>
   ```

3. Don't forget to add the `tfoot` before closing the table!

```
<tfoot>
  <tr>
    <td> </td>
    <td id="sum" class="numeric"> </td>
  </tr>
</tfoot>
</table>
```

4. The following script will sum all of the values in the **Population** column, and display that sum in the table footer:

```
<script type="text/javascript">
  $( document ).ready( function() {
    var sum_population = 0;
    $( "#populationTable tbody tr" ).each( function( index ) {
      sum_population += $( this )children().eq( 1 ).text() * 1;
    });

    $( "td#sum" ).text( sum_population );
  });
</script>
```

Refresh or load the page with the script in place, and you should see a sum in the footer of your table's numeric column:

Country	Population
Canada	34482779
China	1344130000
India	1241491960
Japan	127817277
United States	311591917
	3059513933

How it works...

Start off by declaring a local variable called `sum_population` and set it to 0.

Now look at the selector:

```
$( "#populationTable tbody tr" )
```

This isn't much different than the selector used in the previous recipe, *Table row striping (Must know)*. It's simply selecting all of the table rows within the table body.

With this collection of `<tr>` elements selected, loop over that collection, summing the text of the second `<td>` in each row. You can perform that loop with jQuery's built-in `each()` iterator. `Each()` iterates over a jQuery collection. For each iteration of this loop, add the text in the second `<td>` of the current row.

```
sum_population += $( this ).children().eq( 1 ).text() * 1;
```

The syntax is standard JavaScript shorthand syntax for adding a value to an existing value, and assigning the result to the existing value. In other words, $a = a + b$ is more concisely written as $a += b$.

For each iteration of the loop, `$( this )` is a reference to a `<tr>` element. To get the `<td>` elements that exist within the `<tr>`, use jQuery's `children()` method, which will return the collection of `<td>` elements. Elements at specific index positions within a collection can be referenced via `eq()`, which takes a single integer argument, the index position to select. Remember that jQuery indexes are zero based, so the second `<td>` is at the index position `1`. To get the text from `<td>`, use jQuery's built-in `text()` method.

Because JavaScript is a *typeless* language, it's not uncommon to see 1 + 2 evaluated as 12. "+" is not only the addition operator, but also the concatenation operator. At runtime, JavaScript tries to determine types of variable values. If it determines that they're numeric, it adds them. If it determines that they're strings, it concatenates them. Multiplying the values by 1 removes any ambiguity and firmly establishes to the JavaScript engine that the values are numeric.

Once the iterations are complete, the sum of the values is stored in the `sum_population` variable, which is displayed in the table footer.

```
$( "td#sum" ).text( sum_population );
```

This is a very straightforward selector. Select the `<td>` element with an `id` attribute of "sum". Once that element is found, set the text to the current value of `sum_population`.

There's more...

Each of the `<td>` elements that display the population numbers has a `class` attribute of `numeric`. This was initially done in order to assign a style to those elements and align the text to the right.

It also allows you to use the class name in your selectors. The current selector works just fine, but so would the following, which is arguably cleaner:

```
$( "#populationTable tbody tr td.numeric" )
```

Rather than selecting all of the `<td>` elements by index value, they're now selecting them by class name. This is also safer, as it's not out of the realm of possibility to think that additional columns could be added to the table. Maybe before the "population" column, "latitude" and "longitude" columns are added. Now the "population" column is at index position 3, and the selector is no longer valid.

It's also arguably more efficient as it only selects the specific `<td>` that it needs. The prior code sample selected all the `<td>` elements, and then filtered out those that don't meet a second criteria. Why select something if it's just going to be filtered out?

Show/hide rows (Must know)

Click a link to trigger hiding or displaying of table rows.

Getting ready

Once again, start off with an HTML table. This one is not quite as simple a table as in previous recipes. You'll need to create a few `<td>` tags that span the entire table, as well as provide some specific classes to certain elements.

Last Name	First Name	Phone
Accounting		
Frang	Corey	555-1111
Gonzalez	Scott	555-2222
Resig	John	555-3333
Marketing		
Heberden	Dan	555-4444
Silber	Leah	555-5555
Sontag	Adam	555-6666
Information Technology		
Katz	Yehuda	555-7777
Waldron	Rick	555-8888
Whitbeck	Ralph	555-9999

How to do it...

1. Again, give the table an `id` attribute. Each of the rows that represent a department, specifically the rows that span the entire table, should have a class attribute value of `dept`.

```
<table border="1" id="employeeTable">
<thead>
  <tr>
```

```
          <th>Last Name</th>
          <th>First Name</th>
          <th>Phone</th>
        </tr>
      </thead>
      <tbody>
        <tr>
          <td colspan="3" class="dept">
          </td>
        </tr>
```

2. Each of the department names should be links where the <a> elements have a class
   of `rowToggler`.

   ```
   <a href="#" class="rowToggler">Accounting</a>
   ```

3. Each table row that contains employee data should have a class attribute value that
   corresponds to its department.

> Note that class names cannot contain spaces. So in the case of
> the `Information Technology` department, the class names
> should be `InformationTechnology` without a space. The issue
> of the space will be addressed later.

```
<tr class="Accounting">
  <td>Frang</td>
  <td>Corey</td>
  <td>555-1111</td>
</tr>
```

4. The following script makes use of the class names to create a table whose rows can
   be easily hidden or shown by clicking a link:

   ```
   <script type="text/javascript">
   $( document ).ready( function() {
     $( "a.rowToggler" ).click( function( e ) {
       e.preventDefault();
       var dept = $( this ).text().replace( /\s/g, "" );
       $( "tr[class=" + dept + "]" ).toggle();
     })
   });
   </script>
   ```

5. With the jQuery implemented, departments are "collapsed", and will only reveal the employees when the link is clicked.

Last Name	First Name	Phone
Accounting		
Marketing		
Information Technology		
Katz	Yehuda	555-7777
Waldron	Rick	555-8888
Whitbeck	Ralph	555-9999

How it works...

The jQuery will "listen" for a `click` event on any `<a>` element that has a class of `rowToggler`. In this case, capture a reference to the event that triggered the action by passing e to the click handler function.

```
$( "a.rowToggler" ).click( function( e )
```

In this case, e is simply a variable name. It can be any valid variable name, but e is a standard convention. The important thing is that jQuery has a reference to the event. Why? Because in this case, the event was that an `<a>` was clicked. The browser's default behavior is to follow a link. This default behavior needs to be prevented.

As luck would have it, jQuery has a built-in function called `preventDefault()`. The first line of the function makes use of this by way of the following:

```
e.preventDefault();
```

Now that you've safely prevented the browser from leaving or reloading the page, set a variable with a value that corresponds to the name of the department that was just clicked.

```
var dept = $( this ).text().replace( /\s/g, "" );
```

Most of the preceding line should look familiar. `$( this )` is a reference to the element that was clicked, and `text()` is something you've already used. You're getting the text of the `<a>` tag that was clicked. This will be the name of the department.

But there's one small issue. If the department name contains a space, such as "Information Technology", then this space needs to be removed.

```
.replace( /\s/g, "" )
```

`replace()` is a standard JavaScript function that uses a regular expression to replace spaces with an empty string. This turns "Information Technology" into "InformationTechnology", which is a valid class name.

The final step is to either show or hide any table row with a class that matches the department name that was clicked.

Ordinarily, the selector would look similar to the following:

```
$( "tr.InformationTechnology" )
```

Because the class name is a variable value, an alternate syntax is necessary.

jQuery provides a way to select an element using any attribute name and value. The selector above can also be represented as follows:

```
$( "tr[class=InformationTechnology]" )
```

The entire selector is a literal string, as indicated by the fact that it's enclosed in quotes. But the department name is stored in a variable. So concatenate the literal string with the variable value:

```
$( "tr[class=" + dept + "]" )
```

With the desired elements selected, either hide them if they're displayed, or display them if they're hidden. jQuery makes this very easy with its built-in `toggle()` method.

Highlighting cells (Must know)

Use built-in jQuery traversal methods and selectors to parse the contents of each cell in a table and apply a particular style (for example, a yellow background or a red border) to all cells that meet a specified set of criteria.

Getting ready

Borrowing some data from Tiobe (`http://www.tiobe.com/index.php/content/paperinfo/tpci/index.html`), create a table of the top five programming languages for 2012. To make it "pop" a bit more, each `<td>` in the **Ratings** column that's over 10 percent will be highlighted in yellow, and each `<td>` in the **Delta** column that's less than zero will be highlighted in red. Each `<td>` in the **Ratings** column should have a class of ratings, and each `<td>` in the **Delta** column should have a class of delta.

Additionally, set up two CSS classes for the highlights as follows:

```
.highlight { background-color: #FFFF00; }       /* yellow */
.highlight-negative { background-color: #FF0000; }  /* red */
```

Initially, the table should look as follows:

Position Dec 2012	Position Dec 2011	Programming Language	Ratings Dec 2012	Delta Dec 2011
1	2	C	18.696%	+1.64%
2	1	Java	17.567%	+0.01%
3	5	Objective-C	11.116%	+4.31%
4	3	C++	9.203%	+0.95%
5	4	C#	5.547%	-2.66%

How to do it...

1. Once again, give the table an `id` attribute (but by now, you knew that), as shown in the following code snippet:

```
<table border="1" id="tiobeTable">
<thead>
<tr>
   <th>Position<br />Dec 2012</th>
   <th>Position<br />Dec 2011</th>
   <th>Programming Language</th>
   <th>Ratings<br />Dec 2012</th>
   <th>Delta<br />Dec 2011</th>
</tr>
</thead>
```

2. Apply the appropriate class names to the last two columns in each table row within the `<tbody>`, as shown in the following code snippet:

```
<tbody>
<tr>
   <td>1</td>
   <td>2</td>
   <td>C</td>
   <td class="ratings">18.696%</td>
   <td class="delta">+1.64%</td>
</tr>
```

3. With the table in place and properly marked up with the appropriate class names, write the script to apply the highlights as follows:

```
<script type="text/javascript">
$( document ).ready( function() {
   $( "#tiobeTable tbody tr td.ratings" ).each( function( index ) {
      if ( parseFloat( $( this ).text() ) > 10 ) {
```

```
            $( this ).addClass( "highlight" );
        }
    });

    $( "#tiobeTable tbody tr td.delta" ).each( function( index ) {
        if ( parseFloat( $( this ).text() ) < 0 ) {
            $( this ).addClass( "highlight-negative" );
        }
    });
});
</script>
```

4. Now, you will see a much more interesting table with multiple visual cues:

Position Dec 2012	Position Dec 2011	Programming Language	Ratings Dec 2012	Delta Dec 2011
1	2	C	18.696%	+1.64%
2	1	Java	17.567%	+0.01%
3	5	Objective-C	11.116%	+4.31%
4	3	C++	9.203%	+0.95%
5	4	C#	5.547%	-2.66%

How it works...

The selector for the **Ratings** column is almost identical to the selector used in the *Sum columns (Must know)* recipe. Select the <td> elements within the tbody tag's table rows that have a class of ratings. As with the code in the *Sum columns (Must know)* recipe, use jQuery's each() function to iterate over the collection.

For each iteration of the loop, test whether or not the value (text) of the <td> is greater than 10. Because the values in <td> contain non-numeric characters (in this case, % signs), we use JavaScript's parseFloat() to convert the text to actual numbers:

```
parseFloat( $( this ).text() )
```

Much of that should be review. $(this) is a reference to the element in question. text() retrieves the text from the element. parseFloat() ensures that the value is numeric so that it can be accurately compared to the value 10.

If the condition is met, use addClass() to apply the highlight class to <td>. Do the same thing for the **Delta** column. The only difference is in checking to see if the text is less than zero. If it is, apply the class highlight-negative.

The end result makes it much easier to identify specific data within the table.

Pagination – client side (Should know)

Pressed for space? Don't want to overwhelm your users with too much data at once? Paginate.

Getting ready

For this recipe, we're back to a relatively simple HTML table. No special classes are needed for the purpose of this exercise, as we're going to be focused exclusively on an array of rows within the table. Specifically, rows within the table body.

Ranking	Movie	Release Year
1	Citizen Kane	1941
2	The Godfather	1972
3	Casablanca	1942
4	Raging Bull	1980
5	Singin' in the Rain	1952
6	Gone with the Wind	1939
7	Lawrence of Arabia	1962
8	Schindler's List	1993
9	Vertigo	1958
10	The Wizard of Oz	1939
11	City Lights	1931
12	The Searchers	1956
13	Star Wars	1977
14	Psycho	1960
15	2001: A Space Odyssey	1968

How to do it...

1. As always, create a table with a unique ID. Also for this recipe create a style block to add some formatting as follows:

```
<style type="text/css">
  table, a.paginate { font: normal 75% "Trebuchet MS", Verdana,
Helvetica, Arial, sans-serif; }
  th.ranking { width: 50px; }
  th.title { width: 150px; }
  th.year { width: 100px; }
</style>

<table border="1" id="pagetable">
```

```
<thead>
  <tr>
    <th class="ranking">Ranking</th>
    <th class="title">Movie</th>
    <th class="year">Release Year</th>
  </tr>
</thead>
```

2. Next add some rows in the `tbody` tag:

```
<tbody>
  <tr>
    <td>1</td>
    <td>Citizen Kane</td>
    <td>1941</td>
  </tr>
  <tr>
    <td>2</td>
    <td>The Godfather</td>
    <td>1972</td>
  </tr>
  ...
  <tr>
    <td>15</td>
    <td>2001: A Space Odyssey</td>
    <td>1968</td>
  </tr>
</tbody>
```

3. Pagination wouldn't be worth much without **Previous** and **Next** links. Create a `div` underneath the table to hold each link. Give both links a class of `paginate`, but give each a unique ID as follows:

```
<div>
  <a href="#" class="paginate" id="previous">Previous</a> |
  <a href="#" class="paginate" id="next">Next</a>
</div>
```

4. All that's left is to set up the script. For now page four records at a time:

```
<script type="text/javascript">
$( document ).ready( function() {
  var firstRecord = 0;
  var pageSize = 4;

  var tableRows = $( "#movies tbody tr" );
  $( "a.paginate" ).click( function( e ) {
```

```
      e.preventDefault();

    if ( $( this ).attr( "id" ) == "next" ) {
      if ( firstRecord + pageSize <= tableRows.length ) {
        firstRecord += pageSize;
      }
    } else {
      if ( firstRecord != 0 ) {
        firstRecord -= pageSize;
      }
    }

    paginate( firstRecord, pageSize );
  });

  var paginate = function( startAt, pageSize ) {
    var endAt = startAt + pageSize - 1;

    $( tableRows ).each( function( index ) {
      if ( index >= startAt && index <= endAt ) {
        $( this ).show();
      } else {
        $( this ).hide();
      }
    });
  }

  paginate (firstRecord, pageSize );
});
</script>
```

5. The table is now less overwhelming, and allows the user to page through via **Previous** and **Next** links, as shown in the following screenshot:

Ranking	Movie	Release Year
1	Citizen Kane	1941
2	The Godfather	1972
3	Casablanca	1942
4	Raging Bull	1980
Previous I Next		

How it works...

There's quite a lot happening here. Start off by defining three variables as follows:

- `firstRecord`: All of the table rows will be stored in an array. This variable holds the value, or the array index position, of the row that's currently being displayed at the first position.

- `pageSize`: How many records do we want to display per page? This value is referred to several times in the code, so assigning it to a variable makes it easier to change down the road, should the need arise.

- `tableRows`: A collection of all of the rows in the table. The selector syntax used to select the rows should be familiar by now.

  ```
  $( "#pagetable tbody tr" )
  ```

Next, listen for a `click` event that occurs on an `<a>` element with a class of paginate. This would be both the **Previous** and **Next** links.

```
$( "a.paginate" ).click( function( e )
```

Make sure the browser doesn't try to reload the page or follow the link by preventing the default behavior from occurring. You did this in the *Show/hide rows (Must know)* recipe.

```
e.preventDefault();
```

The next bit of code conditionally checks to see which link was clicked, the **Previous** link or the **Next** link. This is done by checking the `id` attribute. Remember, while each link has the same class name, each link has a unique ID.

```
if ( $( this ).attr( "id" ) == "next" )
```

The first condition fires if the **Next** link is clicked. The `else` obviously fires if the **Previous** link is clicked.

Regardless of which link is clicked, calculate a new value for the `firstRecord` variable. To start, `firstRecord` variable's value is 0. Guard conditions within each of the `Previous` and `Next` conditions ensure that the value of `firstRecord` can neither fall below 0, nor exceed the number of records in the collection.

The guard condition around the **Next** link is as follows:

```
if ( firstRecord + pageSize <= tableRows.length ) {
  firstRecord += pageSize;
}
```

The value of `firstRecord` should never exceed the number of records in the collection. In order to check that clicking on **Next** will not result in that happening, add the value of `pageSize` (currently set to 4) to the value of `firstRecord` (initially 0). As long as that condition is met, a new value can be set for `firstRecord`.

The guard condition around **Previous** is a bit more straightforward:

```
if ( firstRecord != 0 ) {
  firstRecord -= pageSize;
}
```

As long as the user is not on the first page, where the value of `firstRecord` is 0, "activate" the **Previous** link by setting the value of `firstRecord` to be `firstRecord` minus the value of `pageSize`.

If either condition is not met, the existing value of `firstRecord` simply remains unchanged.

With the value of `firstRecord` now properly calculated (either to reflect moving forward or backwards, or staying the same in the case that upper/lower boundaries are exceeded), call a named function, passing in both the calculated value for `firstRecord` as well as `pageSize`.

```
paginate( firstRecord, pageSize );
```

Let's look at that the function a little more closely:

```
var paginate = function( startAt, pageSize ) {
  var endAt = startAt + pageSize - 1;

  $( tableRows ).each( function( index ) {
    if ( index >= startAt && index <= endAt ) {
      $( this).show();
    } else {
      $( this ).hide();
    }
  });
}
```

`paginate()` knows which record to start with, as that value is passed in as an argument to the function. Within the function, the first line calculates the record to end with.

The script has determined which rows to display. It will either be rows 0-3, 4-7, 8-11, or 12-14. Remember that JavaScript is a zero-based system, and the records are being paged four at a time. All of the rows are stored in our `tableRows` variable. You're already familiar with jQuery's `each()` function, as it was used in the *Sum columns (Must know)* and *Highlighting cells (Must know)* recipes. Loop over the table rows and use jQuery's built-in `show()` and `hide()` methods as needed.

```
$( tableRows ).each( function( index ) {
  if ( index >= startAt && index <= endAt ) {
    $( this).show();
  } else {
    $( this ).hide();
  }
});
```

You've used `each()` before, but you haven't yet made use of the `index` variable. `index` simply holds the value of the current iteration of the loop. You're free to name it anything you'd like.

For each iteration of the loop, a conditional runs to determine whether or not the index value of the current element in the collection (the table row) falls in between the `startAt` and `endAt` values.

If the current value of index is within the specified range, display the table row by applying jQuery's `.show()` function.

Otherwise, hide the table row by applying jQuery's `.hide()` function.

Both `show()` and `hide()` are built-in jQuery methods that manipulate an element's display property.

The final line of the script block kicks off the pagination by explicitly calling `paginate()` with a `startAt` value of `0`.

There's more...

This is a fairly simple/straightforward demonstration of client-side pagination. However, it's not particularly user friendly.

For example, it might be nice to disable the **Previous** and **Next** links if the user is at the first or last page within the set.

It also might be nice to display a div above and/or below the table that shows a message, "Now displaying n-m of x records".

But now that we've done the basics, try making the interface a bit more user friendly on your own for extra credit.

Pagination – server side (Should know)

Paginating on the client side, as we did in the previous recipe, is great, but it's not necessarily efficient. If you only want to display four records, why retrieve more than that? If you have a database such as Microsoft SQL Server, MySQL, or PostgreSQL, for example, and a server-side language such as PHP, Ruby, or ASP.NET, you can use jQuery's built-in **AJAX** functions to retrieve specific subsets of data.

We're not going to delve into the server-side code, as that will vary depending on your choice of server-side technologies. Even within a given technology, there are often various frameworks and/or approaches.

What we'll discuss is how to use jQuery on the client side to communicate with your server. I'm going to trust that you'll know how to write the server-side code to query your database and return the appropriate **JSON** data.

Getting ready

For this recipe, start off with the simplest table of all. Use the same data as in the previous recipe, but start off with a completely empty table body. Keep the **Previous** and **Next** links, as they'll still be needed.

How to do it...

1. Create the table with an ID of your choice. Leave the `tbody` tag empty. On the initial page load, an AJAX call will retrieve data from the server, and populate the rows within the `tbody`.

```
<table border="1">
<thead>
  <tr>
    <th class="ranking">Ranking</th>
    <th class="title">Movie</th>
    <th class="releaseYear">Release Year</th>
  </tr>
</thead>
<tbody>
</tbody>
</table>
```

2. Reuse the same **Previous** and **Next** links that were used in the previous recipe:

```
<div>
  <a href="#" class="paginate" id="previous">Previous</a> |
  <a href="#" class="paginate" id="next">Next</a>
</div>
```

3. Finally, add the script. Continue to page four records at a time.

```
<script type="text/javascript">
$( document ).ready( function() {
  var firstRecord = 0;
  var pageSize = 4;

  var recordcount = $.ajax({
    type: "GET",
    url: "_recordcount.php",
    async: false
```

```
        }).responseText;

      $( "a.paginate" ).click( function( e ) {
        e.preventDefault();

        if ( $( this ).attr( "id" ) == "next" ) {
          if ( firstRecord + pageSize <= recordcount ) {
            firstRecord += pageSize;
          }
        } else {
          if ( firstRecord != 0 ) {
            firstRecord -= pageSize;
          }
        }

        paginate( firstRecord, pageSize );
      });

      var paginate = function( startAt, pageSize ) {
        $( "#movies tbody tr" ).remove();

        $.ajax({
          type: "POST",
          url: "_paginate.php",
          data: { startAt: firstRecord, pageSize: pageSize },
          dataType: "json"
        }).done( function( data ) {
          $.each( data, function( index, val ) {
            var tablerow = "<tr><td>" + val[ 0 ] + "</td><td>" +
              val[ 1 ] + "</td><td>" + val[ 2 ] + "</td></tr>";
            $( "#movies tbody" ).append( tablerow );
          });
        });
      }

      paginate( firstRecord, pageSize );
    });
</script>
```

4. The table should initially load with the first four records displayed, even though the table markup was empty:

Ranking	Movie	Release Year
1	Citizen Kane	1941
2	The Godfather	1972
3	Casablanca	1942
4	Raging Bull	1980
Previous I Next		

How it works...

Once again, there's quite a lot happening here, but some of it should be familiar from the previous recipe.

Let's start by defining three variables:

- **firstRecord**: All of the table rows will be stored in an array. This variable holds the value, or the array index position, of the row that's currently being displayed at the first position. This is exactly the same as in the previous recipe.

- **pageSize**: How many records do we want to display per page? This value is referred to several times in the code, so assigning it to a variable makes it easier to change down the road, should the need arise. This is exactly the same as in the previous recipe.

- **recordcount**: In the previous recipe, there was a variable called `tablerows`, which held the number of rows in the table. That was used to ensure that the user didn't try to page past the number of total rows. But since the data is being retrieved only as it's needed, the total number of table rows isn't immediately known. So make the first of two `$.ajax()` calls. Take a closer look at the `$.ajax()` call before moving on:

```
var recordcount = $.ajax({
  type: "GET",
  url: "_recordcount.php",
  async: false
}).responseText;
```

`$.ajax()` is a built-in jQuery function. The options being used here are as follows:

- `type: "GET"` – No data is being posted, just `GET` the `recordcount`.
- `URL:` – This is the page that jQuery will interact with.
- `async: false` – Because the result of this AJAX call is being assigned to a variable, it should not happen asynchronously. If it does, there is a risk of trying to reference the variable before the value is set.

The AJAX call returns an object. Among the properties returned is the `responseText`. That's the specific value that is assigned to the `recordcount` variable.

Now that the total number of records is known, continue.

The next section handles the `click` events on the **Previous** and **Next** links. This block remains unchanged from the previous recipe. Simply calculate the `firstRecord` variable for the next set of records, and call the `paginate()` function.

The `paginate()` function itself is rather different than in the previous recipe, but still fairly straightforward.

The first thing to do is to remove all of the table rows within the table body. On initial page load, there are none, but subsequent calls to the function will have some displayed. Removing the rows is accomplished using jQuery's built-in `remove()` method.

```
$( "#movies tbody tr" ).remove();
```

Now for another AJAX call, this time to retrieve the records. It's similar to the first AJAX call with a couple of notable exceptions. First, it's doing a `POST` rather than a `GET`, because data is being sent to the server. That data is the `startAt` value and the `pageSize` value. Because JSON is being sent back, specify that as the **dataType**.

The returned data will look as follows (taken from Firefox's Firebug plugin):

```
Headers   Post   Response   HTML

[["1","Citizen Kane","1941"],["2","The Godfather","1972"],["3","Casablanca","1942"],["4","Raging Bull"
,"1980"]]
```

This is an array of arrays. Loop over that data manually, and construct the table rows to be displayed.

This looping is done via the `.done()` method, which is built into the `$.ajax()` object. The `done()` method has a hook into the data that was returned from the AJAX call. Being the creative sort, I refer to that in the code as data. This is just a variable name, however. You can name it whatever you like. In this case, `movierecords` might have been a more descriptive name.

Loop over that array data via jQuery's `$.each()` function. You've seen something similar before, where `.each()` was used to iterate over a jQuery collection. In this case, it's not a reference to a specific jQuery object or collection, but a generic iterator that's part of jQuery itself. In fact, the `$` in front of it is a direct reference to jQuery.

`$.each()` takes two arguments. The object that will be iterated over, and a callback function that holds an index variable and a variable reference to the current item:

```
$.each( data, function( index, val )
```

For each loop iteration, create a table row with three table cells. The value of each cell will be `val[ 0 ]`, `val[ 1 ]`, and `val[ 2 ]`. Remember that the arrays are zero-based. The constructed table row is then assigned to a variable, `tablerow` (yes, once again, creatively named).

```
var tablerow = "<tr><td>" + val[ 0 ] + "</td><td>" + val[ 1 ] + "</
td><td>" + val[ 2 ] + "</td></tr>";
```

The final step is to append the newly constructed table row into the table body of the table. `.append()` is another built-in jQuery function that, surprisingly enough, appends an element into an existing element.

```
$( "#movies.tbody" ).append( tablerow );
```

That's it for the function. All that's left to do is to call it on initial page load, and four rows should appear in the table.

There's more...

While it's much nicer to only retrieve the specific records to display, this can still be cleaned up a bit. As with client-side paging, you might want to disable the **Previous** and **Next** links when the user is at the lower or upper boundaries of the `recordset`.

Additionally, we show a great deal of faith that our server will be up and running, and that our server-side code will be error free. As with the `.done()` method, `$.ajax()` also has a built-in `.error()` method that will fire if something unexpected should occur. It's probably a good idea to make use of this and be prepared for the worst.

Column sorting – client side (Should know)

Add interactivity to your HTML tables by allowing users to sort table columns.

Getting ready

Stick with the table of the top 15 movies that's been used a few times already. Unlike the last recipe, where we started with an empty table body, this time we'll populate all 15 rows.

Ranking	Movie	Release Year
1	Citizen Kane	1941
2	The Godfather	1972
3	Casablanca	1942
4	Raging Bull	1980
5	Singin' in the Rain	1952
6	Gone with the Wind	1939
7	Lawrence of Arabia	1962
8	Schindler's List	1993
9	Vertigo	1958
10	The Wizard of Oz	1939
11	City Lights	1931
12	The Searchers	1956
13	Star Wars	1977
14	Psycho	1960
15	2001: A Space Odyssey	1968

How to do it...

1. Start with the same table that was used in the past few recipes. Because columns will be sorted by clicking on the headers, add `<a>` elements to the table header text. Each `<a>` element should have a class of sorter and a unique ID, `column_n`, where n is the number of the column in the table, starting at `0`.

```
<table border="1" id="movies">
<thead>
  <tr>
    <th class="ranking">
      <a href="#" class="sorter" id="column_0">Ranking</a>
    </th>
    <th class="title">
      <a href="#" class="sorter" id="column_1">Movie</a>
    </th>
    <th class="releaseYear">
      <a href="#" class="sorter" id="column_2">Release Year</a>
    </th>
  </tr>
</thead>
```

2. Manually enter all of the movies into rows in the `tbody`, as follows:

```
<tbody>
<tr>
  <td>1</td>
  <td>Citizen Kane</td>
  <td>1941</td>
</tr>
<tr>
  <td>2</td>
  <td>The Godfather</td>
  <td>1972</td>
</tr>
...
<tr>
  <td>15</td>
  <td>2001: A Space Odyssey</td>
  <td>1968</td>
</tr>
</tbody>
```

3. Finally, add the sorting script, as follows:

```
<script type="text/javascript">
$( document ).ready( function() {
  var tablerows = $( "#movies tbody tr" ).get();

  $( "a.sorter" ).click( function( e ) {
    e.preventDefault();

    $( "#movies tbody tr" ).remove();

    // on which column are we sorting?
    var sort_pos = $( this ).attr( "id" ).split( "_" )[ 1 ];

    tablerows.sort( function( a, b ) {
      var atext = $( a ).children( "td" ).eq (sort_pos ).text();
      var btext = $( b ).children( "td" ).eq( sort_pos ).text();

      var nums_only = /^\d+$/;
      if ( nums_only.test( atext ) ) atext *= 1;
      if ( nums_only.text( btext ) ) btext *= 1;

      if ( atext == btext ) return 0;
      return atext < btext ? -1 : 1;
    });

    $.each( tablerows, function( index, tablerow ) {
      $( "#movies tbody" ).append( tablerow );
    });
  });

});
</script>
```

How it works...

The first thing to do is to get an array of the table rows. Once again, jQuery makes this ridiculously simple with its built-in `get()` function. Assign this array to a variable, since it will be referenced later.

```
var tablerows = $( "#movies tbody tr" ).get();
```

The selector itself should be familiar by now. The only thing that's new is the addition of `.get()`, which will create an array of the elements retrieved.

Each of the table headers is surrounded by an `<a href>` tag with a class attribute of `sorter`. Listen for a `click` event on those elements to kick off the function:

```
$( "a.sorter" ).click( function( e ) {
```

Because a link was clicked, prevent the default behavior via `e.preventDefault()`. This was used in previous recipes, so it should be familiar.

As in the previous recipe, clear out all of the table rows within the table body. They'll be added back once they're properly sorted. But before that is done, they need to be removed.

```
$( "#movies.tbody tr" ).remove();
```

Now it starts to get a little bit trickier. Determine which column should be sorted. Each of the header links contains a unique ID whose value has a very specific format: `column_n`, where `n` is the index of the column. Start the index at 0, so there are IDs `column_0`, `column_1`, and `column_2`.

This specific format will allow you to get the ID via `$( this ).attr( "id" )`. You can then use JavaScript's built-in `split()` function to explode the string into an array. `split()` takes a string argument, which is the substring or pattern on which to split the original string. Use the underscore character to create the array. Because the ID values are all in the `column_n` format, `split()` will result in a two element array. The first element, which is at the 0 position, will hold the literal string `column`. The second element, which is at the 1 position, will hold the column number.

```
var sort_pos = $( this ).attr( "id" ).split( "_" )[ 1 ];
```

`sort_pos` now holds the value 0, 1, or 2, for this table.

Now for the actual `sort`. `JavaScript` provides a `.sort()` method that works on arrays. This isn't jQuery, but standard JavaScript. It's a pretty straightforward algorithm that looks as follows:

```
array.sort( function( a, b ) {
  if ( a == b ) return 0;
  if ( a < b ) return -1;
  if ( a > b ) return 1;
}
```

Kick off the sort function on the `tablerows` array as follows:

```
tablerows.sort( function( a, b ) {
```

Unfortunately, that can't be used directly. The array holds table rows. Table row `a` can't be compared to table row `b`. The text is in a specific `td` within table row `a` and table row `b`.

```
var atext = $( a ).children( "td" ).eq( sort_pos ).text();
var btext = $( b ).children( "td" ).eq( sort_pos ).text();
```

Since both a and b reference specific table rows, drill down into that table row to a specific `<td>`, and grab the text using jQuery's `.text()` method.

`$( a )` and `$( b )` are jQuery hooks into the table rows being compared. This returns an array of the child `td` elements via `.children( "td" )`, but a specific `td` is needed. Remember that a variable `sort_pos` was set earlier? This is where it gets implemented. Having traversed down to the appropriate `td` element, use `.text()` to get its value.

Now run the comparisons for the sort algorithm, but use `atext` and `btext` rather than a and b.

```
if ( atext == btext ) return 0;
if ( atext < btext ) return -1;
if ( atext > btext ) return 1;
```

With that, the `tablerows` array is properly sorted. Loop over it and append each row back into the table body:

```
$.each( tablerows, function(index, tablerow) {
  $( "#movies tbody" ).append( tablerow );
});
```

There's more...

Note that if the **Ranking** column is sorted, the results are not 1,2,3,....,15 as one might expect. Rather, the results are 1,10,11,12,13,14,15,2,3,...9. This is also a result of JavaScript being a typeless language. JavaScript is seeing the values as strings, and the string 10 comes before the string 2.

It's a bit of a kludge, but you can do a test to see if the values being compared are numeric. If they are, multiply them by 1. This will leave the value unchanged, but let JavaScript know that these are numeric values.

Prior to the comparison, do the following:

```
var nums_only = /^\d+$/;
```

The `nums_only` variable is a regular expression that checks for one or more digits. Then use JavaScript's native `.test()` method to test the values. If they're true, multiply the value by 1. This will address the issue of sorting the numeric values.

```
if ( nums_only.test( atext ) ) atext *= 1;
if ( nums_only.test( btext ) ) btext *= 1;
```

This sort only sorts in one direction. Take this opportunity to allow a column heading to be clicked and re-sort the column in the opposite direction. If it was ascending, now sort it in descending order, and vice versa. As a hint, store some variables to allow you to determine which column is currently sorted, and in which direction. Then re-sort in the opposite direction, which would involve a small change to the sort algorithm.

Column sorting – server side (Should know)

With a reasonably-sized record set, client-side table sorting is a nice option. But if there are too many records, browsers might buckle under the strain. In those cases, let the server do the work and sort with AJAX.

As with the previous recipe that dealt with AJAX, we won't delve into the server-side code. I trust that you've got your favorite server-side language and database, and know how to set them up.

Getting ready

The initial setup for this chapter is exactly the same as it was for the previous recipe. Stick with the table of top movies. Assume a database table with columns **Ranking**, **Movie**, and **Release Year**.

Ranking	Movie	Release Year
1	Citizen Kane	1941
2	The Godfather	1972
3	Casablanca	1942
4	Raging Bull	1980
5	Singin' in the Rain	1952
6	Gone with the Wind	1939
7	Lawrence of Arabia	1962
8	Schindler's List	1993
9	Vertigo	1958
10	The Wizard of Oz	1939
11	City Lights	1931
12	The Searchers	1956
13	Star Wars	1977
14	Psycho	1960
15	2001: A Space Odyssey	1968

How to do it...

1. As usual, create a table with a unique ID. As with the previous recipe, clicking the column headings will sort, but this time it's going to be a server-side sort. To simplify the server-side code, give each column ID values that correspond with the database column name. Continue to use `class="sorter"` for all of the headings.

```
<table border="1" id="movies">
<thead>
  <tr>
    <th>
      <a href="#" class="sorter" id="ranking">Ranking</a>
    </th>
    <th>
      <a href="#" class="sorter" id="movie">Movie</a>
    </th>
    <th>
      <a href="#" class="sorter" id="releaseYear">Release Year</a>
    </th>
  </tr>
</thead>
```

2. The `tbody` will contain all 15 movie rows, the same as in the previous recipe.

3. The script will be notably different, since we're now going out to the server to retrieve the sorted records.

```
<script type="text/javascript">
  $( document ).ready( function() {

    $( "a.sorter" ).click( function( e ) {
      e.preventDefault();

      $( "#movies tbody tr" ).remove();

      $.ajax({
        type: "POST",
        url: "_sort.php",
        data: { orderby: $( this ).attr( "id" ) },
        dataType: "json"
      }).done( function( data ) {
        $.each( data, function( index, val ) {
          var tablerow = "<tr><td>" + val[ 0 ] + "</td><td>" +
            val[ 1 ] + "</td><td>" + val[ 2 ] + "</td></tr>";
```

```
            $( "#movies tbody" ).append( tablerow );
        });
    });
});

});
</script>
```

How it works...

Since there's absolutely nothing new about the table or markup, let's jump right into the script. Much of this should be just review, as there's nothing in this script that hasn't already been covered. Trigger the sort when a link with class sorter is clicked.

```
$( "a.sorter" ).click( function( e ) {
```

As you know by now, prevent the default behavior so that the browser doesn't try to follow the link and/or reload the page.

Jumping right into the $.ajax() call. You've done an AJAX post before, where you sent startAt and pageSize as data. In this recipe, send a variable called orderby, which is the value of the id attribute of each of the links in the column headers. This is accessible via $(this).attr("id").

The .done() method that's baked into jQuery's $.ajax() is also something that has already been used. In fact, the entire body of the .done() method is identical here to the body of the .done() method in the *Pagination – server side (Should know)* recipe. Use jQuery's built-in $.each() iterator to loop over the results. With each iteration of the loop, construct a table row, and use .append() to append it to the tbody of the table.

The only real difference between the AJAX call in the *Pagination – server side (Should know)* recipe and the AJAX call here is what happens on the server. In the *Pagination – server side (Should know)* recipe, a specific subset of records was retrieved, which I did via mySQL's LIMIT directive.

For sorting, we're merely doing an ORDER BY in the SQL. The value of the ORDER BY is the value that passed as data in the $.ajax() call.

This should be pretty consistent among most databases.

For my setup using PHP and mySQL, the relevant code from `_sort.php` is as follows:

```
$orderby = $_POST[ "orderby" ];
$result = mysql_query( "SELECT `ranking`,`movie`,`releaseYear` FROM
`movies` ORDER BY $orderby" );

$data = array();

while ( $row = mysql_fetch_row( $result ) ) {
   $data[] = $row;
}

echo json_encode($data);
```

As in the previous recipe, this sort only sorts in one direction. It should be a little bit easier to modify this one to be able to reverse the sort if a specific column head is clicked on twice. You'll still need to store a variable locally in order to know which column is sorted and in which direction, but there will be no need to modify the sort algorithm. There is none! Simply pass an "ASC" or "DESC" as part of the data to the `$.ajax()` call. It might look something similar to the following:

```
$.ajax({
          type: "POST",
          url: "_sort.php",
          data: { orderby: $( this ).attr( "id" ), direction: "ASC"
             },
          dataType: "json"
       })
```

A small modification to the server-side code to sort the ORDER BY in a particular direction is the only change needed.

Filtering (Become an expert)

Paging and sorting a table adds interactivity to your site, and can help your users locate specific bits of information. But if they know what they're looking for, rather than having to page or sort, it would be efficient to give them a filter field.

Getting ready

We've come to love it, so stick with the table of movies. This time, underneath the table, add a form field.

Ranking	Movie	Release Year
1	Citizen Kane	1941
2	The Godfather	1972
3	Casablanca	1942
4	Raging Bull	1980
5	Singin' in the Rain	1952
6	Gone with the Wind	1939
7	Lawrence of Arabia	1962
8	Schindler's List	1993
9	Vertigo	1958
10	The Wizard of Oz	1939
11	City Lights	1931
12	The Searchers	1956
13	Star Wars	1977
14	Psycho	1960
15	2001: A Space Odyssey	1968

Release Year: [   ]

How to do it...

1. You should be able to bang out this particular table code in your sleep, so we'll forego displaying that code. But underneath the table, add a form field as follows:

```
<div>
    Release Year: <input type="text" name="filter" id="filter" />
</div>
```

2. The script will let users filter the release year. As they type into the form field, the `keyup` event will trigger the jQuery function, which will hide any rows that don't contain the text input by the user:

```
<script type="text/javascript">
$( document ).ready( function() {

  $( "input#filter" ).keyup( function() {
    var filtertext = $( this ).val();

    $( "#movies tbody tr" ).each( function( rowindex ) {
      $( this ).children( "td" ).eq( 2 ).each( function(
        cellindex ) {
        if ( $( this ).text().indexOf( filtertext ) < 0 ) {
          $( this ).parents( "tr" ).hide();
        } else {
          $( this ).parents( "tr" ).show();
        }
      });
    });
  })

});
</script>
```

How it works...

Start off by listening for a `keyup` event this time, rather than the `click` event that has been used in previous recipes. It's implemented the same way:

```
$( "input#filter" ).keyup( function() {
```

The first thing to do is to store the input in a local variable:

```
var filtertext = $( this ).val();
```

Now compare that text with the text in the **Release Year** column. To accomplish this, use two `.each()` loops.

The first loop will iterate over all of the rows in the `tbody`:

```
$( "#movies tbody tr" ).each( function( rowindex ) {
```

With each loop over the table rows, then loop over each `td` at index position 2. Say it with me, indexes start at 0, so position 2 is column 3.

```
$( this ).children( "td" ).eq( 2 ).each( function( cellindex ) {
```

With each iteration of the inner loop, compare the text in the `td` element to the text in the filter input. As long as the text in the `td` contains a substring of the text in the filter input, display it. For example, 193 would display 1932 and 1939, but would hide 1940, 1941, and so on. Do this with JavaScript's `indexOf()` function. `indexOf()` checks for the existence of a substring within a string. If the substring is not found, it returns `-1`. Otherwise, it returns the starting position of the first instance of the substring. For now, know that if the value returned is less than 0, the substring was not found, so hide the row.

```
if ( $( this ).text().indexOf( filtertext ) < 0 ) {
    $( this ).parents( "tr" ).hide();
} else {
    $( this ).parents( "tr" ).show();
}
```

Beyond just hiding rows that don't meet the criteria, use `.show()` to display rows that do, as they may have been hidden before, but now meet the filter criteria.

Filter functions can be very powerful. This was just a basic example of how to demonstrate the concept. You could have iterated over every table cell, or given the user a drop-down menu to select the column on which they want to filter. You also could have provided a submit button that filtered only when the button was clicked, rather than on each keyup.

Plugins (Should know)

I know what you've been thinking all this time. "Charlie, why do I need to know how to do these things when there are so many plugins available for jQuery?" That's a very good question.

There are numerous plugins available for jQuery, and specifically for table manipulation. Sometimes the plugins are overkill, though. Maybe a particular plugin doesn't work exactly the way you'd like it to. Perhaps your employer is shy about using third-party code (except, of course, for jQuery itself).

Plugins are great, and they are a significant part of the reason that jQuery is so popular. It's always good to know how to do something on your own, though. Of course once you know how, it never hurts to work smarter, and not harder.

There are two table-related plugins that I generally use when the need arises: **tablesorter** (`http://tablesorter.com/docs/`) and **DataTables** (`http://www.datatables.net/`).

Getting ready

For both tablesorter and DataTables, download the plugins to your server and call them from your pages. You still need to include jQuery, as the plugins assume you have jQuery set up properly.

After downloading the `.js` files from the URLs listed above, add appropriate link's paths to your page's `<head>` section. For example:

```
<script type="text/javascript" src="/path/to/jquery.tablesorter.min.
js"></script>
<script type="text/javascript" src="/path/to/jquery.datatables.min.
js"></script>
```

Some plugins also offer `.css` files, which will be needed to achieve a particular look and feel. We'll forego the aesthetics and dive right into functional implementation.

How to do it...

1. Both tablesorter and DataTables can be applied to any well-marked up HTML table. As per usual, assume a table with an ID of `movies`.

2. To apply tablesorter to the table, add the following script to the bottom of the page:

```
<script type="text/javascript">
  $( document ).ready( function() {
    $( "#movies" ).tablesorter();
  });
</script>
```

3. To apply DataTables to the table, add the following script to the bottom of the page:

```
<script type="text/javascript">
  $( document ).ready( function() {
    $( "#movies" ).dataTable();
  });
</script>
```

4. It may be worth pointing out that you would apply one plugin or the other to your `#movies` table, but not both!

How it works...

For basic functionality, there's very little magic. Simply include the scripts as shown and the rest just works. That's the beauty of the extensible jQuery plugin architecture.

You might not notice any significant changes to the appearance of your table with either plugin. Although with DataTables you'll see some extra goodies around the table, such as a dropdown to display "n" records, a filter form field, and Previous/Next links for pagination. See the following screenshot for reference:

Ranking	Movie	Release Year
1	Citizen Kane	1941
2	The Godfather	1972
3	Casablanca	1942
4	Raging Bull	1980
5	Singin' in the Rain	1952
6	Gone with the Wind	1939
7	Lawrence of Arabia	1962
8	Schindler's List	1993
9	Vertigo	1958
10	The Wizard of Oz	1939

Show 10 entries
Search:

Showing 1 to 10 of 15 entries
PreviousNext

Both tablesorter and DataTables include CSS files with their downloads. Include them into the page in much the same way that you included the .js files, and you will have tables that are not only functional but also aesthetically pleasing.

Add the following line to your tablesorter page:

```
<link rel="stylesheet" href="tablesorter.css" type="text/css"
media="print, projection, screen" />
```

The preceding code yields the following table:

Ranking	Movie	Release Year
1	Citizen Kane	1941
2	The Godfather	1972
3	Casablanca	1942
4	Raging Bull	1980
5	Singin' in the Rain	1952
6	Gone with the Wind	1939
7	Lawrence of Arabia	1962
8	Schindler's List	1993
9	Vertigo	1958
10	The Wizard of Oz	1939
11	City Lights	1931
12	The Searchers	1956
13	Star Wars	1977
14	Psycho	1960
15	2001: A Space Odyssey	1968

Likewise, add the following line of code to your DataTables page:

```
<link rel="stylesheet" href="dataTables.css" type="text/css"
media="print, projection, screen" />
```

The preceding code yields the following table:

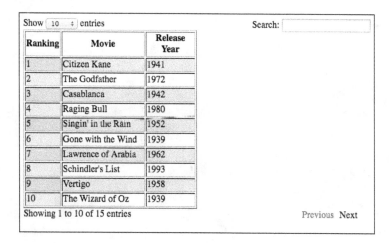

Both downloads include additional stylesheets as well as images, such as up/down arrows for column headers to indicate sorting. Additionally, you can tweak the styles as you see fit.

As impressive as the out-of-the-box functionality may be, both plugins also offer a number of options.

Tablesorter shows a number of examples at `http://tablesorter.com/docs/#Examples`. They include forcing a default sort order, appending table data with AJAX, and sorting fields that contain markup (for example, ignoring the markup and sorting on the text).

DataTables examples are located at `http://www.datatables.net/examples/`. While by default both tablesorter and DataTables can be utilized in a single line of code, and while they both have various options, DataTables is insanely configurable.

No disrespect to tablesorter. It essentially does one thing, and it does it well. If table sorting is all that you need, DataTables may be overkill. But for a Swiss army knife of table-related functionality, DataTables is impressive.

Thank you for buying
Instant jQuery 2.0 Table Manipulation How-to

About Packt Publishing

Packt, pronounced 'packed', published its first book *"Mastering phpMyAdmin for Effective MySQL Management"* in April 2004 and subsequently continued to specialize in publishing highly focused books on specific technologies and solutions.

Our books and publications share the experiences of your fellow IT professionals in adapting and customizing today's systems, applications, and frameworks. Our solution based books give you the knowledge and power to customize the software and technologies you're using to get the job done. Packt books are more specific and less general than the IT books you have seen in the past. Our unique business model allows us to bring you more focused information, giving you more of what you need to know, and less of what you don't.

Packt is a modern, yet unique publishing company, which focuses on producing quality, cutting-edge books for communities of developers, administrators, and newbies alike. For more information, please visit our website: www.packtpub.com.

Writing for Packt

We welcome all inquiries from people who are interested in authoring. Book proposals should be sent to author@packtpub.com. If your book idea is still at an early stage and you would like to discuss it first before writing a formal book proposal, contact us; one of our commissioning editors will get in touch with you.

We're not just looking for published authors; if you have strong technical skills but no writing experience, our experienced editors can help you develop a writing career, or simply get some additional reward for your expertise.

jQuery UI 1.8: The User Interface Library for jQuery

ISBN: 978-1-84951-652-5   Paperback: 424 pages

Build highly interactive web applications with ready-to-use widgets from the jQuery User Interface Library

1. Packed with examples and clear explanations of how to easily design elegant and powerful front-end interfaces for your web applications

2. A section covering the widget factory including an in-depth example on how to build a custom jQuery UI widget

3. Updated code with significant changes and fixes to the previous edition

Learning jQuery 1.3

ISBN: 978-1-84719-670-5   Paperback: 444 pages

Better Interaction Design and Web Development with Simple JavaScript Techniques

1. An introduction to jQuery that requires minimal programming experience

2. Detailed solutions to specific client-side problems

3. For web designers to create interactive elements for their designs

4. For developers to create the best user interface for their web applications

5. Packed with great examples, code, and clear explanations

6. Revised and updated version of the first book to help you learn jQuery

Please check **www.PacktPub.com** for information on our titles